Expression

Gideon Stanford

Presentation by *BookLeaf Publishing*

Web: www.bookleafpub.com

E-mail: info@bookleafpub.com

ISBN: 9789357740302

First edition 2023

To whom it may concern.

31:10-31

Walking down a familiar way,
Past a field of buttercups,
A spot of difference caught my eye,
Which made me stay my steps.

Mixed among the other flowers,
A single rose took root,
And pierced the sea of yellow
With its dark and reddish hue.

The beauty of the buttercups
Lay in their uniformity,
But the beauty of the rose:
Her disinterest in conformity.

At first I thought to leave the rose,
But as I looked I longed to take it;
To pluck it from its place
And pin it to my pocket.

Nevertheless I left it there,
Against my heart's desire,
To seek the owner of the field
And about the rose inquire.

So I did.
And my request he half obliged,
But required one thing of me:
That I return to ask another time.

And so return I will,
If nothing keeps me here.
For such a rose as her,
I could wait at least another year.

Meanwhile, as I wait,
I walk often past that place
To visit the fair red rose
And see the beauty of her face.

False Originality?

"No thought at all is ever an original."
At least, that's what I've been told.
"A new thought, who can think?" They say.
But, for some odd reason,
I keep thinking anyway.

I think lots of thoughts,
And I hope they think much of me.
Like a babbling brook, never ceasing to flow,
So are my thoughts:
As one comes, another goes.

Some I like, others I don't.
My mind seems not to care.
Sometimes,
As if having a mind of its own,
It shows me things I wish I'd not been shown.

But the important thoughts are those I think on
purpose;
The ones which I need strain to conceive,
And require some effort on my part.
These are those that bring forth revelation;
Those which bring forth art.

Yet, of course, these mean nothing.
For who can think up something new?
At least, that's a stance some like to take.
But, who can really know if a thought is new or
not?
I suppose none can truly say.

Gravity

A friend have I who leaves me not
(Though some days I wish she would).
A grounding force she is for sure.
I'd escape her 'er I could.

Up and out and around I'd go,
In orbit above the world.
Yet still I think she'd follow me there.
Yes. Live I with her for good.

Some have gone and felt not her pull,
Yet it be still there.
But all have come back at terminal speed
And kissed her where they were.

As for me, stuck here am I,
Likely to never break free.
Though, maybe someday I'll get the chance,
Someday–maybe–we'll see.

Icicles

There hangs from my roof quite a curious group:
Spires of all shapes and sizes.
Through the crack 'neath my door, my ears hear
still more.
Their presence is all except silent.

A musical sound running down to the ground,
A droplet on the tip of each one;
Then falling fast the drips hit with a splash,
Melting, creating a song.

Reflecting their Maker, in step with all nature,
This choir of spires sings softly aloud.
Their tune is for any who pause enough to
listen–
Those kinds are this choir's crowd.

Preserved

7

Layers upon layers,
Leafy branches stretch high and low–
A vast sea of greenery
In which stands, alone, one large trunk:
Strong, straight, beautiful,
Reaching towards the heavens,
Tied to the ground.

Piccadilly Fairies

Piccadilly fairies can be
Very, very hairy,
But these fairly hairy fairies
Keep their hairy heads in check.

*Read With An M.L.E. Accent

Dust Devil,
Let me check your levels.
Got attacked by the Shovel Shriveler.
No, mama, I won't take none ya mana.
Mañana, let me get away.

Gone creepin'.
Won't be catchin' feelin's.
Snuck a bite out my brothers sandwich.
Late lunch,
Early dinner.
Still hungry.
Let me catch a break.

Spunky Sailor
Went to see the jailor,
Took a two year sabbatical to the Badlands.
Times up.
Time to drop the mop.
Sailor man's lost in the waves.

Whatcha got?
Won't be gettin' shot.
Take a photo somewhere else.

Not today.
What did I just say?
Get that camera out my face.

Pea Sized Service

I met some fleas
Who bake bread for peas
Since peas cannot bake for themselves.
Such noble fleas
Never have I seen,
Nor thought peas should need to eat.

As it turns out, they do.
It's true! Who knew?
And fleas make talented bakers.
They mix and knead
And portion the dough,
But not to the scale that we're used to.

Headspace

I had given some thought to my thoughts over
the years,
But the thought I had given them was not much
at all.
Though, once I had thought about the thoughts I
was having
(and of such I had not thought for a while),
my slinky, thinky thoughts became far less
clingy,
And the loudest of my thoughts, I think,
Became far less clinky.

If I'm Being Honest

I hate to write about
My gloomy inner strife;
To load another's heart
With the troubles of my life.

But what honest alternative exists
If strife is what I own?
To write of something else
Would leave the truth untold.

And truth is what I seek to tell.
Dishonest words are of no use–
Vain and coarse they seem to me,
But trust and hope does truth produce.

So I write against my want
About the gunk inside.
Though, what that is I haven't said.
It seems the truth I mean to hide.

Words Fail, He Doesn't

Words are too weak.
A week's worth of words wouldn't do.
Language fails me.
My thoughts remain unexpressed,
Repressed within the caverns of my soul.

Tell me, am I blind?
For the one thing I seek
Remains the only thing I cannot find.
Or, am I deaf?
Do my words return empty?
Are my cries for help an unintelligible waste of
breath?

Far be it from me to believe such lies,
For the One to whom I call has faithfully
answered time after time.
He hears my cry and acts quickly on my behalf.
He it is who made the heart in my chest.

Wordplay

Let's play with words;
Thoughtlessly throw them around,
Mix-up their meanings,
Flip their up-sides down.

Let's use some so often
That they lose all meaning,
And put a ban on some
To spare others' feelings.

Let's diminish their definitions.
For example: "brave" should mean "loud",
"Love" should mean "lust",
And "correct"–up to the crowd.

Let's make new words
On behalf of other people.
Not for their sake,
But to make us feel like heroes.

Let's mumble, and jumble
All the words together
So that in the confusion,
We're pushed farther apart than ever.

And when push comes to shove,
So we're in need of diplomacy,
The weapons that were our words
Will be dull, useless things.

And angry people
Armed with useless words
Know violence is better
Than to try to be heard.

Cause to be heard means nothing
If words can't convey meaning,
But violence speaks volumes
To all those receiving.

Two Thirds Across

Still, damp air;
A cold, muggy atmosphere.
Plunging down,
A steep ravine.
Shooting up,
Great, dark trees.
One, Two, Three–
People gathered in the mist.

One, two
One, two.
One foot, then the other.
One, two,
One, two.
One's across the fallen tree.

Two, three,
Two, slip, catch.
Pause a moment. Take a breath.
Two, three,
Two, three.
An outstretched arm,
hands hold tight.
Two's across the narrow beam.

Three, four,
Three, four.
One step, then one more.
Three, four,
Three, slip.
An outstretched arm,
an empty hand.
One, Two, Three's no more.

Plunging down, a steep ravine.
Shooting up above the trees,
A single soul:
One of Three.

Habitual Creature

19

My cat sits in a ditch; in a divot in the ground.
Why, I ask, does my cat sit there?
He's there when I come home–every time I
come home.
When I see him, he runs away.
When he runs away, I don't see him.
Why does my cat sit there, in the divot; in the
ditch?

Wait For What?

Our house cat likes to wait at my open window.
Often, do I see her there.
For what she waits, I do not know;
Neither does she care to share.

New, Perfect

There's a place I know in my mind;
A peaceful place with the same feeling each
time.
I can't control when I go,
But when I am there I know it.
I can't paint with paint or I'd paint a picture and
show it.
How's this? I'll paint a picture with words;
A picture so clear you'll forget that you heard it
And thought you saw it instead.
Now listen, picture this:

In one word: Heaven.
But not with the old guy and Cherubim.
No, this Heaven's on earth–
New earth, new Heaven.
A Heavenly earth so perfectly molded for man
You feel like you can reach out and touch it,
But you can't.

You can't touch it,
But you can feel there and be there;
See, smell, hear, breath there.
You feel like you died and came back to life–
Maybe you're sleeping.

Sometimes "awake" is hard to define.

It's hard to describe where only I've been,
But maybe, if I try hard enough,
You'll begin to get it, and then
Brick by brick this metaphor will form
A picture of the place I've known since I was
born.

Heaven on earth: this place is vast.
It's much like our earth,
Except the new earth's not trashed
With all the junk we drag out to the curb in a
can.
But that's not the point, this is:
The new earth remains unstained by man.

The sin of man's hands has left our earth
scarred,
Species extinct, the atmosphere charred.
But in the new Heaven's descension on the new
earth, watch,
The air you breathe there is the literal presence
of God.

His presence so real, so pure, and so tangible,
The air you exhale is the eternal
Praise of the only Name under Heaven
By which anyone must be saved–

Saved from sin and death and pain.
And when you're there he wipes every tear from
your face.
But you're never there long enough to get a
good look.
It's like as soon as you start reading,
He closes the book.

A Handmade Chasm

Looking out, hoping to feel within.
Feeling within, wishing to shut my eyes.
A shovel lies on the rim of a chasm.
One side of the abyss: what I feel.
The other: what I know.
Yet, there's a muddy line, drawn in the sand,
Between my want and my desire.
Clarity, clouded by chemistry–
Peace, thwarted by immaturity.
Half dormant emotions bubble to the surface,
The bubbles bursting into tidal waves of
longing,
Longing so swiftly forgotten.
Hypocrisy is a wretched friend.
Discipline brandishes a rod.
One knows where to find peace and security,
But my vision is impaired by Ignorance,
Who clamors for my attention.

9:27 PM

25

A lengthy poem would I write,
With meaning as the stars,
And depth as a woman's heart,
Were it not so late at night.

The Hour Glass

Sand runs down
In a constant stream,
Yet at the top
No change is seen.
Until all of the sudden,
A slight divot appears,
And slowly grows
As on go the years.
Then, seemingly,
Out of somewhere,
The last grain falls
And hits the others
Making no sound at all.
The half, once full,
Is now fully emptied.
And the half, once empty,
Finds fullness anew.

Forgotten Is Fine

27

The notepad I carry is battered and bent,
The pages are creased and half of them spent.
The pen in my pocket is low on ink.
The brain in my head struggles to think.

The ideas I write down have been written
before;
They've been presented by another with far
better form.
Someday, the pen in my pocket will write its last
dot
And the notepad I carry will be lost and forgot.

But that's okay, far as I'm concerned.
My words don't need to be kept or remembered.
I simply enjoy writing them down.
The process is what I care most about.

P.S.

I washed it;
Left it in my pocket.
My notepad's no more,
But I think that's ironic.